A ROOKIE BIOGRAPHY

JOHN CHAPMAN

The Man Who Was Johnny Appleseed

By Carol Greene

CHILDRENS PRESS®
CHICAGO

This book is for Andrew and Rebecca Shipp.

John Chapman (1774-1845)

Library of Congress Cataloging-in-Publication Data

Greene, Carol.
    John Chapman : (the man who was Johnny Appleseed) / by Carol
Greene.
        p. cm. — (A Rookie biography)
    Includes index.
    Summary: Relates how John Chapman's distribution of apple seeds and
trees across America made him a legend.
    ISBN 0-516-04223-8
    1. Appleseed, Johnny, 1774-1845—Juvenile literature. 2. Apple
growers—United States—Biography—Juvenile literature. 3. Frontier and
pioneer life—Middle West—Juvenile literature. [1. Appleseed, Johnny,
1774-1845. 2. Apple growers. 3. Frontier and pioneer life.] I. Title.
II. Series: Greene, Carol. Rookie biography.
SB63.C46G74   1991
634′.11′092—dc20
[B]   91-12649
                                                         CIP
                                                          AC

John Chapman was
a real person.
He lived from 1774 to 1845.
During his life, he
planted many apple trees.
That is why people
call him Johnny Appleseed.
This is his story.

TABLE OF CONTENTS

Apple trees have beautiful blossoms.

Chapter 1

A Mystery Story

John Chapman's early life
is like a mystery story.
We don't know much about it.

But we do know that
John was born on
September 26, 1774, in
Leominster, Massachusetts.

Some people say
apple trees were
blooming that day.
But that's silly.
Apple trees don't
bloom in September.

John and his family
lived in a poor little house.
Soon his father went off
to fight England in
the Revolutionary War.

Poster calling for colonists to join George Washington's army

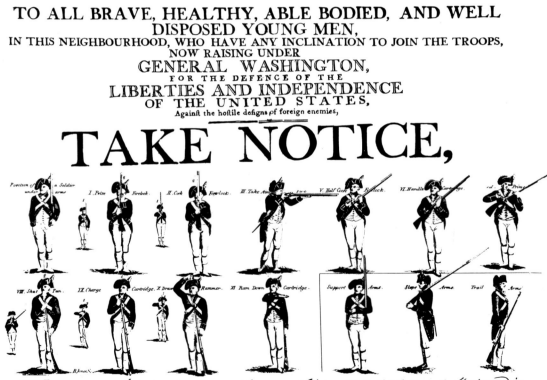

TO ALL BRAVE, HEALTHY, ABLE BODIED, AND WELL
DISPOSED YOUNG MEN,
IN THIS NEIGHBOURHOOD, WHO HAVE ANY INCLINATION TO JOIN THE TROOPS,
NOW RAISING UNDER
GENERAL WASHINGTON,
FOR THE DEFENCE OF THE
LIBERTIES AND INDEPENDENCE
OF THE UNITED STATES,
Against the hostile designs of foreign enemies,

TAKE NOTICE,

THAT _____ Tuesday, Wednesday Thursday, Friday and Saturday at Spotswood in _____ county, attendance will be given by Middlesex Recruiting with his music and recruiting party of _____ company in. _____ Battalion of the 11th regiment of infantry, commanded by Lieutenant Colonel Aaron Ogden, for the purpose of receiving the enrollment of such youth of SPIRIT, as may be willing to enter into this HONOURABLE service.

The ENCOURAGEMENT at this time, to enlist, is truly liberal and generous, namely, a bounty of TWELVE dollars, an annual and fully sufficient supply of good and handsome cloathing, a daily allowance of a large and ample ration of provisions, together with SIXTY dollars a year in GOLD and SILVER money on account of pay, the whole of which the soldier may lay up for himself and friends, as all articles proper for his subsistance and comfort are provided by law, without any expence to him.

Those who may favour this recruiting party with their attendance as above, will have an opportunity of hearing and seeing in a more particular manner, the great advantages which these brave men will have, who shall embrace this opportunity of spending a few happy years in viewing the different parts of this beautiful continent, in the honourable and truly respectable character of a soldier, after which, he may, if he pleases return home to his friends, with his pockets FULL of money and his head COVERED with laurels.

GOD SAVE THE UNITED STATES.

Before John was two,
his mother died.
His grandparents may have
taken care of him and
his big sister Elizabeth.
No one knows for sure.

When his father, Nathaniel,
came back from the war,
he had a new wife, Lucy.
By then, John was six.

John may have gone to live
with Nathaniel and Lucy
in a tiny old house in
Longmeadow, Massachusetts.
No one knows that
for sure either.

But we do know
that the house soon
became crowded.
Nathaniel and Lucy
had ten children.

We also know that
somehow, somewhere,
John learned to
read and write.

He learned to love nature
and to feel at home
in the forests
and on the water.

And that is almost all
we know about John
until he was 23.

Wyoming Forest in Pennsylvania

Chapter 2

The First Trip

One November day in 1797,
John set off across
the mountains in Pennsylvania.

He carried a sack
with some food and
some apple seeds in it.
John's feet were bare,
but his heart was happy.

For a while, the sun shone
down on the mountain forests.
John walked almost 100 miles.
Then, all at once,
it began to snow.

It snowed and snowed.
By the time it stopped,
the snow was three feet deep.

John made camp
in a safe place.
He tore cloth from
the bottom of his coat
and tied it around his feet.

He made snowshoes from
the branches of beech trees.
Then he traveled on.

By spring, he was near
Warren, Pennsylvania.
There, next to a river,
John planted some apple seeds.

Not many settlers had come to
northwest Pennsylvania yet.
But John knew they would soon
come—and when they did,
they would need apple trees.

Settlers chopped down trees to build their homes in the wilderness.

The apple press (right) was used to make cider. Settlers ate the apples from John Chapman's trees.

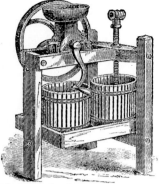
Settlers cooked apples into apple butter and applesauce. They used them to make apple cider. They traded apples for other things.

OCTOBER.

Clearing the land was hard work.

So John went from
one place to another,
clearing land
and planting his apple seeds.
He built a fence of brush
around each little nursery.

At least once a year, he
checked on his nurseries.
By the time settlers came,
he was ready to sell
or trade his young apple trees.

From then on,
this was John's job,
and, after a while,
people began to call him
Johnny Appleseed.

John Chapman planted apple seeds in
Pennsylvania, Ohio, and Indiana.

Chapter 3

The Ohio Years

By 1800, John had
traveled into Ohio.
Some of the settlers there
were pretty rough.
But John got along with
just about everybody.

By 1809, he had a
string of nurseries growing
in Ohio and Pennsylvania.
They took a lot of work
and a lot of traveling, but
John didn't mind.

The summer of 1812 brought
Indian attacks in Ohio.
No one could blame the
Native Americans. They
had been treated badly.

John Chapman
got along well with
the Native Americans.
But he didn't want
anyone to be killed.

Before the Indians attacked, John went from cabin to cabin and warned all the settlers.

John worked in
north-central Ohio
for about 20 years.
He bought some land
and he rented some, too.
Mostly he traveled.

Sometimes he slept in
a nest made of leaves
in a log or a hollow tree.
He loved to lie on his back
and look at the stars.

"It seems almost as though
I can see the angels
praising God," he said,
"for He has made
all things for good."

John often ate corn mush
or potatoes that he
roasted in his campfire.
He didn't like to kill
animals for food—
or for any other reason.

But once he had to kill a
rattlesnake that bit him.

"I am sorry for it," said John
with tears in his eyes.

Once when he saw mosquitoes
flying into his campfire
and burning up,
John put out the fire
and sat there in the cold.

Sometimes settlers turned
their old horses loose
in the forests to die.
John found the horses
and paid other people
to take care of them.

John liked children, too.
He told them stories
about his adventures.
He gave them ribbons,
beads, and pretty cloth.

He met a boy named
David Hunter. David was 16
when his parents died.
He had to take care of
eight little brothers and sisters.

John gave David 60 trees
to start an apple orchard.
David worked hard and
his orchard grew
to over 600 trees.

John gave apple trees
to other poor people, too.
And he went on planting.

Chapter 4

A Strange-Looking Old Man

John didn't care what he wore.
He was always clean, but
he often looked strange.

Sometimes he wore old clothes
that other people gave him.
Sometimes he had to tie his
shoes to his feet with string.
Sometimes he went barefoot.

One man said John's feet
looked like elephant skin.

John might wear an old
soldier's hat on his head.
He might wear a hat
he had made out of cardboard.
He might even wear the pot
he used to cook his corn mush.

Greenfield, Indiana

By 1828, John had gone west
through Ohio to Indiana.
Some of the land he saw
was wet and swampy.
But John knew settlers
would come before long.

So he went on planting.

After a while, he got
to know the settlers.
Sometimes he stayed
with them in their cabins.
But he almost always slept
on the floor by the fire.

John liked to tell folks
about his religion.
He'd come in, lie down,
open his Bible, and say,
"Fresh news right from Heaven."

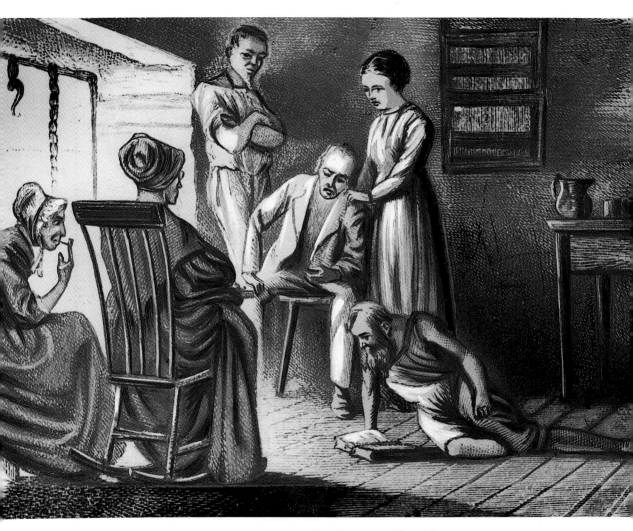

John Chapman, sitting on the floor, would read
the Bible to the settlers he visited.

Years went by.
One day John heard
that cattle had broken
into one of his nurseries
near Fort Wayne, Indiana.
He hurried off to save the trees.

His friends, the Worths,
had a cabin nearby.
John stayed with them.
But he was worn out
and caught fever.

John Chapman died
at the Worth cabin around
March 17 or 18, 1845.
No one is quite sure when.

It would be nice to think that apple trees
bloomed the day John Chapman died.

Some people say
apple trees were
blooming that day.
But that's silly.
Apple trees don't
bloom in the middle of March.

John was buried
in a nearby cemetery.
No one is quite sure where.

But later, people put up
a gravestone so no one would
forget Johnny Appleseed.
The words on the stone say,
"He lived for others."

Chapter 5

Tales and More Tales

People began telling
tales about John while
he was still alive.
After all, he was different
from most other folks.

Some people said he could
thaw ice with his bare feet.
Some said he went barefoot
to punish his feet for
stepping on a worm.

Others made up sad love stories.
They couldn't figure out why
John never got married.

The tales that were told
got bigger and bigger
after John died.

Some say he planted
apple trees all the way
to the Pacific Ocean.
Some say his ghost
comes to the forest when
someone needs help.

One tale turned John
into a poet and a fiddler.

People wrote books and plays,
and poems and songs about him.
He was the star of a cartoon.
Ohio named a highway for him.

None of John's apple trees
are alive anymore.
But some of them lived
for a very long time.
Trees from *their* seeds
could still be alive.

Do you think
these trees and
apples grew from
the seeds left
by the trees
John Chapman
planted so long ago?

Johnny Appleseed
might like that better
than any tale.

Important Dates

1774   September 26—Born in Leominster, Massachusetts, to Nathaniel and Elizabeth Chapman

1780   May have moved to Longmeadow, Massachusetts

1797   Left for northwest Pennsylvania

1800   Traveled into Ohio

1812   Worked as scout, warning Ohio settlers of Indian attacks

1828   Went as far as Fort Wayne, Indiana

1845   Died near Fort Wayne, Indiana (probably March 17 or 18)

INDEX

Page numbers in boldface type indicate illustrations.

PHOTO CREDITS

ABOUT THE AUTHOR

Carol Greene has degrees in English literature and musicology. She has worked
in international exchange programs, as an editor, and as a teacher of writing.
She now lives in Webster Groves, Missouri, and writes full-time. She has
published more than 100 books, including those in the Rookie Biographies series.